T0333422

NEW SELECTED POEMS

DEREK MAHON

New Selected Poems

Gallery Books

ff

FABER & FABER

First published in 2016
by Faber & Faber Ltd
The Bindery, 51 Hatton Garden
London
and
The Gallery Press
Loughcrew, Oldcastle, County Meath, Ireland

Edited by Peter Fallon and originated by The Gallery Press
Printed by Imprint Digital, Exeter

A CIP record for this book is available from the British Library

ISBN 978-0-571-33156-7

Our authorised representative in the EU for product safety is
Easy Access System Europe, Mustamäe tee 50, 10621 Tallinn, Estonia
gpsr.requests@easproject.com

17

Contents

for Sarah

Glengormley

'Wonders are many and none is more wonderful than man'
who has tamed the terrier, trimmed the hedge
and grasped the principle of the watering can.
Clothes pegs litter the window ledge
and the long ships lie in clover; washing lines
shake out white linen over the chalk thanes.

Now we are safe from monsters, and the giants
who tore up sods twelve miles by six
and hurled them out to sea to become islands
can worry us no more. The sticks
and stones that once broke bones will not now harm
a generation of such sense and charm.

Only words hurt us now. No saint or hero,
landing at night from the conspiring seas,
brings dangerous tokens to the new era —
their sad names linger in the histories.
The unreconciled, in their metaphysical pain,
dangle from lamp posts in the dawn rain;

and much dies with them. I should rather praise
a worldly time under this worldly sky —
the terrier-taming, garden-watering days
those heroes pictured as they struggled through
the quick noose of their finite being. By
necessity, if not choice, I live here too.

Carrowdore

(at the grave of Louis MacNeice)

Your ashes will not stir, even on this high ground,
however the wind tugs, the headstones shake.
This plot is consecrated, for your sake,
to what lies in the future tense. You lie
past tension now, and spring is coming round
igniting flowers on the peninsula.

Your ashes will not fly, however the winds roar
through yew and bramble. Soon the biographies
and buried poems will begin to appear,
but we pause here to remember the lost life.
Maguire proposes a blackbird in low relief
over the grave, and a phrase from Euripides.

Which suits you down to the ground, like this churchyard
with its play of shadow, its humane perspective.
Locked in the winter's fist, these hills are hard
as nails, yet soft and feminine in their turn
when fingers open and the hedges burn.
This, you implied, is how we ought to live —

the ironical, loving crush of roses against snow,
each fragile, solving ambiguity. So
from the pneumonia of the ditch, from the ague
of the blind poet and the bombed town you bring
the all-clear to the empty holes of spring,
rinsing the choked mud, keeping the colours new.

Day Trip to Donegal

We reached the sea in early afternoon,
climbed stiffly out; there were things to be done,
clothes to be picked up, friends to be seen.
As ever, the nearby hills were a deeper green
than anywhere in the world, and the grave
grey of the sea the grimmer in that enclave.

Down at the pier the boats gave up their catch,
a squirming glimmer of gills. They fetch
ten times as much in the city as there,
and still the fish come in year after year —
herring and mackerel, flopping about the deck
in attitudes of agony and heartbreak.

We left at eight, drove back the way we came,
the sea receding down each muddy lane.
Around midnight we changed down into suburbs
sunk in a sleep no gale-force wind disturbs.
The time of year had left its mark
on frosty pavements glistening in the dark.

Give me a ring, goodnight, and so to bed . . .
That night the slow sea washed against my head,
performing its immeasurable erosions —
spilling into the skull, marbling the stones
that spine the very harbour wall,
muttering its threat to villages of landfall.

At dawn I was alone far out at sea
without skill or reassurance — nobody
to show me how, no promise of rescue —
cursing my constant failure to take due
forethought for this; contriving vain
overtures to the vindictive wind and rain.

An Unborn Child

(for Michael and Edna Longley)

I have already come to the verge of
departure; a month or so and
I shall be vacating this familiar room.
Its fabric fits me almost like a glove
while leaving latitude for a free hand.
I begin to put on the manners of the world
sensing the splitting light above
my head, where in the silence I lie curled.

Certain mysteries are relayed to me
through the dark network of my mother's body
while she sits sewing the white shrouds
of my apotheosis. I know the twisted
kitten that lies there sunning itself
under the bare bulb, the clouds
of goldfish mooning around upon the shelf.
In me these data are already vested;

I know them in my bones — bones which embrace
nothing, for I am completely egocentric.
The pandemonium of encumbrances
which will absorb me, mind and senses,
intricacies of the maze and the rat race,
I imagine only. Though they linger and,
like fingers, stretch until the knuckles crack,
they cannot dwarf the dimensions of my hand.

I must compose myself at the nerve centre
of this metropolis, and not fidget —
although sometimes at night, when the city
has gone to sleep, I keep in touch with it,
listening to the warm red water
racing in the rivers of my mother's body;

or the moths, soft as eyelids, or the rain
wiping its wet wings on the windowpane.

And sometimes, too, in the small hours of the morning
when the dead filament has ceased to ring,
after the goldfish are dissolved in darkness
and the kitten has gathered itself up into a ball
between the groceries and the sewing,
I slip the trappings of my harness
to range these hollows in discreet rehearsal
and, kicking at the concavity of my caul,

produce in my mouth the words 'I want to live!' —
this my first protest, and shall be my last.
As I am innocent, everything I do
or say is couched in the affirmative.
I want to see, hear, touch and taste
these things with which I am to be encumbered.
Perhaps I needn't worry. Give
or take a day or two, my days are numbered.

An Image from Beckett

In that instant
there was a sea, far off,
as bright as lettuce,

a northern landscape
and a huddle
of houses along the shore.

Also, I think, a white
flicker of gulls
and washing hung to dry —

the poignancy of those
back yards! — and the gravedigger
putting aside his forceps.

Then the hard boards
and darkness once again.
But in that instant

I was struck
by the sweetness and light,
the sweetness and light,

imagining what grave
cities, what lasting monuments,
given the time.

They will have buried
our great-grandchildren, and theirs,
beside us by now

with a subliminal batsqueak
of reflex lamentation.
Our knuckle bones

litter the rich earth
changing, second by second,
to civilizations.

It was good while it lasted,
and if it only lasted
the Biblical span

required to drop six feet
through a glitter of wintry light,
there is No One to blame.

Still, I am haunted
by that landscape,
the soft rush of its winds,

the uprightness of its
utilities and schoolchildren —
to whom in my will,

this, I have left my will.
I hope they have time,
and light enough, to read it.

Lives

(for Seamus Heaney)

First time out
I was a torc of gold
and wept tears of the sun.

That was fun
but they buried me
in the earth two thousand years

till a labourer
turned me up with a pick
in eighteen fifty-four.

Once I was an oar
but stuck in the shore
to mark the place of a grave

when the lost ship
sailed away. I thought
of Ithaca, but soon decayed.

The time that I liked
best was when
I was a bump of clay

in a Navaho rug,
put there to mitigate
the too god-like

perfection of that
merely human artifact.
I served my maker well —

he lived long
to be struck down in
Denver by an electric shock

the night the lights
went out in Europe
never to shine again.

So many lives,
so many things to remember!
I was a stone in Tibet,

a tongue of bark
at the heart of Africa
growing darker and darker . . .

It all seems
a little unreal now,
now that I am

an anthropologist
with my own
credit card, dictaphone,

army-surplus boots
and a whole boatload
of photographic equipment.

I know too much
to be anything any more;
and if in the distant

future someone
thinks he has once been me
as I am today,

let him revise
his insolent ontology
or teach himself to pray.

Afterlives

(for James Simmons)

I

I wake in a dark flat
to the soft roar of the world.
Pigeons neck on the white
roofs as I draw the curtains
and look out over London
rain-fresh in the morning light.

This is our element, the bright
reason on which we rely
for the long-term solutions.
The orators yap, and guns
go off in a back street;
but the faith doesn't die

that in our time these things
will amaze the literate children
in their non-sectarian schools
and the dark places be
ablaze with love and poetry
when the power of good prevails.

What middle-class shits we are
to imagine for one second
that our privileged ideals
are divine wisdom, and the dim
forms that kneel at noon
in the city not ourselves.

2

I am going home by sea
for the first time in years.
Somebody thumbs a guitar
on the dark deck, while a gull
dreams at the masthead,
the moon-splashed waves exult.

At dawn the ship trembles, turns
in a wide arc to back
shuddering up the grey lough
past lightship and buoy,
slipway and dry dock
where a naked bulb burns;

and I step ashore in a fine rain
to a city so changed
by five years of war
I scarcely recognize
the places I grew up in,
the faces that try to explain.

But the hills are still the same
grey-blue above Belfast.
Perhaps if I'd stayed behind
and lived it bomb by bomb
I might have grown up at last
and learnt what is meant by home.

Leaves

The prisoners of infinite choice
have built their house
in a field below the wood
and are at peace.

It is autumn, and dead leaves
on their way to the river
scratch like birds at the windows
or tick on the road.

Somewhere there is an afterlife
of dead leaves,
a forest filled with an infinite
rustling and sighing.

Somewhere in the heaven
of lost futures
the lives we might have led
have found their own fulfilment.

A Curious Ghost

While your widow clatters water into a kettle
you lie at peace in your tropical grave —
a sea captain who died at sea, almost.
Lost voyager, what would you think of me,
husband of your fair daughter but impractical?
You stare from the mantelpiece, a curious ghost
in your peaked cap, as we sit down to tea.
The bungalows still signal to the sea,
rain wanders the golf course as in your day,
the river still flows past the distillery
and a watery sun shines on Portballintrae.

I think we would have had a lot in common —
alcohol and the love of one woman
certainly; but I failed the eyesight test
when I tried for the Merchant Navy,
and lapsed into this lyric lunacy.
When you lost your balance like Li Po
they found unfinished poems in your sea-chest.

The Snow Party

(for Louis Asekoff)

Bashō, coming
to the city of Nagoya,
is asked to a snow party.

There is a tinkling of china
and tea into china;
there are introductions.

Then everyone
crowds to the window
to watch the falling snow.

Snow is falling on Nagoya
and farther south
on the tiles of Kyōto;

eastward, beyond Irago,
it is falling
like leaves on the cold sea.

Elsewhere they are burning
witches and heretics
in the boiling squares,

thousands have died since dawn
in the service
of barbarous kings;

but there is silence
in the houses of Nagoya
and the hills of Ise.

The Last of the Fire Kings

I want to be
like the man who descends
at two milk churns

with a bulging
string bag and vanishes
where the lane turns,

or the man
who drops at night
from a moving train

and strikes out over the fields
where fireflies glow,
not knowing a word of the language.

Either way I am
through with history —
who lives by the sword

dies by the sword.
Last of the fire kings, I shall
break with tradition and

die by my own hand
rather than perpetuate
the barbarous cycle.

Five years I have reigned
during which time
I have lain awake each night

and prowled by day
in the sacred grove
for fear of the usurper,

perfecting my cold dream
of a place out of time,
a palace of porcelain

where the frugivorous
inheritors recline
in their rich fabrics
far from the sea.

But the fire-loving
people, rightly perhaps,
will not countenance this,

demanding that I inhabit,
like them, a world of
sirens, bin-lids
and bricked-up windows —

not to release them
from the ancient curse
but to die their creature and be thankful.

The Mayo Tao

I have abandoned the dream kitchens for a low fire
and a prescriptive literature of the spirit;
a storm snores on the desolate sea.
The nearest shop is four miles away.
When I walk there through the shambles
of the morning for tea and firelighters
the mountain paces me in a snow-lit silence.
My days are spent in conversation
with deer and blackbirds;
at night fox and badger gather at my door.
I have stood for hours
watching a trout doze in the tea-gold dark,
for months listening to the sob story
of a stone in the road — the best,
most monotonous sob story I have ever heard.

I am an expert on frost crystals
and the silence of crickets, a confidant
of the stinking shore, the stars in the mud —
there is an immanence in these things
which drives me, despite my scepticism,
almost to the point of speech,
like sunlight cleaving the lake mist at morning
or when tepid water
runs cold at last from the tap.

I have been working for years
on a four-line poem
about the life of a leaf;
I think it might come out right this winter.

Ford Manor

Even on the quietest days the distant
growl of cars remains persistent,
reaching us in this airy box
we share with the fieldmouse and the fox;
but she drifts in maternity blouses
among crack-paned greenhouses —
a pregnant Muse in love with life,
part child, part mother, and part wife.

Even on the calmest nights the fitful
prowl of planes is seldom still
where Gatwick tilts to guide them home
from Tokyo, Nice, New York or Rome;
yet even today the earth disposes
bluebells, roses and primroses,
the dawn throat-whistle of a thrush
deep in the dripping lilac bush.

The Banished Gods

Paros, far-shining star of dark-blue Earth,
   reverts to the sea its mother.
      The tiny particles,
    sand grains and marble dust,
panic into the warm brine together.

Near the headwaters of the longest river
   there is a forest clearing,
     a dank, misty place
    where light stands in columns
and birds sing with a noise like paper tearing.

Far from land, far from the trade routes,
   in an unbroken dream time
     of penguin and whale
    the seas sigh to themselves
reliving the days before the days of sail.

Down a dark lane at the back of beyond
   a farm dog lies by a dead fire
     dreaming of nothing
    while a window goes slowly grey
brightening a laid table and hung clothing.

Where the wires end the moor seethes in silence,
   scattered with scree, primroses,
     feathers and faeces;
    it shelters the hawk and hears
in dreams the forlorn cries of lost species.

It is here that the banished gods are in hiding,
   here they sit out the centuries
     in stone, water
    and the hearts of trees,
lost in a reverie of their own natures —

of zero-growth economics and seasonal change
   in a world without cars, computers
      or nuclear skies,
   where thought is a fondling of stones
and wisdom a five-minute silence at moonrise.

A Refusal to Mourn

He lived in a small farmhouse
at the edge of a new estate.
The trim gardens crept
to his door, and car engines
woke him before dawn
on dark winter mornings.

All day there was silence
in the bright house. The clock
ticked on the kitchen shelf,
cinders moved in the grate,
and a warm briar gurgled
when the old man talked to himself;

but the doorbell seldom rang
after the milkman went,
and if a shirt-hanger
knocked in an open wardrobe
that was a strange event
to contemplate for hours

while the wind thrashed about
in the back garden, raking
the tin roof of the hen-house,
and swept clouds and gulls
eastwards over the lough
with its flap of tiny sails.

Once a week he would visit
an old shipyard crony,
inching down to the road
and the blue country bus
to sit and watch sun-dappled
branches whipping the windows

while the long evening shed
weak light in his empty house,
on the photographs of his dead
wife and their six children
and the Missions to Seamen angel
in flight above the bed.

'I'm not long for this world,'
said he on our last evening,
'I'll not last the winter,'
and grinned, straining to hear
whatever reply I made;
and died the following year.

In time the astringent rain
of those parts will clean
the words from his gravestone
in the crowded cemetery
that overlooks the sea
and his name be mud once again

and his boilers lie like tombs
in the mud of the sea bed
till the next ice age comes
and the earth he inherited
is gone like Neanderthal Man
and no records remain.

But the secret bred in the bone
on the dawn strand survives
in other times and lives,
persisting for the unborn
like a claw-print in concrete
after the bird has flown.

A Disused Shed in Co. Wexford

Let them not forget us, the weak souls among the asphodels.
— Seferis, *Mythistorema*

(for J. G. Farrell)

Even now there are places where a thought might grow —
Peruvian mines, worked out and abandoned
to a slow clock of condensation,
an echo trapped for ever, and a flutter
of wildflowers in the lift-shaft,
Indian compounds where the winds dance
and a door bangs with diminished confidence,
lime crevices behind rippling rain barrels,
dog corners for bone burials;
and in a disused shed in Co. Wexford,

deep in the grounds of a burnt-out hotel,
among the bathtubs and the washbasins
a thousand mushrooms crowd to a keyhole.
This is the one star in their firmament
or frames a star within a star.
What should they do there but desire?
So many days beyond the rhododendrons
with the world revolving in its bowl of cloud,
they have learnt patience and silence
listening to the rooks querulous in the high wood.

They have been waiting for us in a foetor
of vegetable sweat since civil war days,
since the gravel-crunching, interminable departure
of the expropriated mycologist.
He never came back, and light since then
is a keyhole rusting gently after rain.
Spiders have spun, flies dusted to mildew
and once a day, perhaps, they have heard something —

a trickle of masonry, a shout from the blue
or a lorry changing gear at the end of the lane.

There have been deaths, the pale flesh flaking
into the earth that nourished it;
and nightmares, born of these and the grim
dominion of stale air and rank moisture.
Those nearest the door grow strong —
'Elbow room! Elbow room!'
The rest, dim in a twilight of crumbling
utensils and broken pitchers, groaning
for their deliverance, have been so long
expectant that there is left only the posture.

A half century, without visitors, in the dark —
poor preparation for the cracking lock
and creak of hinges; magi, moonmen,
powdery prisoners of the old regime,
web-throated, stalked like triffids, racked by drought
and insomnia, only the ghost of a scream
at the flash-bulb firing squad we wake them with
shows there is life yet in their feverish forms.
Grown beyond nature now, soft food for worms,
they lift frail heads in gravity and good faith.

They are begging us, you see, in their wordless way,
to do something, to speak on their behalf
or at least not to close the door again.
Lost people of Treblinka and Pompeii!
'Save us, save us,' they seem to say,
'Let the god not abandon us
who have come so far in darkness and in pain.
We too had our lives to live.
You with your light meter and relaxed itinerary,
let not our naive labours have been in vain!'

Going Home

(for John Hewitt)

I am taking leave of the trees,
the beech, the cedar, the elm,
the mild woods of these parts
misted with car exhaust
and sawdust, and the last
gasps of the poisoned nymphs.

I have watched girls walking
and children playing under
lilac and rhododendron,
and me flicking my ash
into the rose bushes
as if I owned the place;

as if the trees responded
to my ignorant admiration
before dawn when the branches
glitter at first light,
or later when the finches
disappear for the night;

and often thought if I lived
long enough in this house
I would turn into a tree
like somebody in Ovid
— a small tree certainly
but a tree nevertheless —

perhaps befriend the oak,
the chestnut and the yew,
become a home for birds,

a shelter for the nymphs,
and gaze out over the downs
as if I belonged here too.

But where I am going the trees
are few and far between —
no richly forested slopes,
not for a long time,
and few winking woodlands.
There are no nymphs to be seen.

Out there you would look in vain
for a rose bush; but find,
rooted in stony ground,
a last stubborn growth
battered by constant rain
and twisted by the sea wind

with nothing to recommend it
but its harsh tenacity
between the blinding windows
and the forests of the sea,
as if its very existence
were a reason to continue.

Crone, crow, scarecrow,
its worn fingers scrabbling
at a torn sky, it stands
on the edge of everything
like a burnt-out angel
raising petitionary hands.

Grotesque by day, at twilight
an almost tragic figure
of anguish and despair,

it merges into the funeral
cloud continent of night
as if it belongs there.

The Chinese Restaurant in Portrush

Before the first visitor comes the spring
softening the sharp air of the coast
in time for the first seasonal 'invasion'.
Today the place is as it might have been,
gentle and almost hospitable. A girl
strides past the Northern Counties Hotel,
light-footed, swinging a book bag,
and the doors that were shut all winter
against the north wind and the sea mist
lie open to the street, where one
by one the gulls go window-shopping
and an old wolfhound dozes in the sun.

While I sit with my paper and prawn chow mein
under a framed photograph of Hong Kong
the proprietor of the Chinese restaurant
stands at the door as if the world were young,
watching the first yacht hoist a sail
— an ideogram on sea cloud — and the light
of heaven upon the hills of Donegal;
and whistles a little tune, dreaming of home.

North Wind

I shall never forget the wind
on this benighted coast.
It works itself into the mind
like the high keen of a lost
Lear spirit in agony
condemned for eternity

to wander cliff and cove
without comfort, without love.
It whistles off the stars
and the existential, stark
face of the cosmic dark.
We crouch to roaring fires.

Yet there are mornings when,
even in midwinter, sunlight
flares, and a rare stillness
lies upon roof and garden —
each object eldritch-bright,
the sea scarred but at peace.

Then, from the ship we say
is the lit town where we live
(our whiskey-and-forecast world),
a smaller ship that sheltered
all night in the restless bay
will weigh anchor and leave.

What did they think of us
during their brief sojourn?
A string of lights on the prom
dancing mad in the storm —
who lives in such a place?
and will they ever return?

The shops open at nine
as they have always done,
the wrapped-up bourgeoisie
hardened by wind and sea.
The newspapers are late
but the milk shines in its crate.

Everything swept so clean
by tempest, wind and rain!
Elated, you might believe
that this was the first day —
a false sense of reprieve,
for the climate is here to stay.

So best prepare for the worst
that chaos and old night
can do to us: were we not
raised on such expectations,
our hearts starred with frost
through many generations?

Prospero and his people never
came to these stormy parts;
few do who have the choice.
Yet, blasting the subtler arts,
that weird, plaintive voice
sings now and for ever.

Courtyards in Delft

— Pieter de Hooch, 1659

(for Gordon Woods)

Oblique light on the trite, on brick and tile —
immaculate masonry, and everywhere that
water tap, that broom and wooden pail
to keep it so. House-proud, the wives
of artisans pursue their thrifty lives
among scrubbed yards, modest but adequate.
Foliage is sparse, and clings; no breeze
ruffles the trim composure of those trees.

No spinet-playing emblematic of
the harmonies and disharmonies of love,
no lewd fish, no fruit, no wide-eyed bird
about to fly its cage while a virgin
listens to her seducer, mars the chaste
perfection of the thing and the thing made.
Nothing is random, nothing goes to waste.
We miss the dirty dog, the fiery gin.

That girl with her back to us who waits
for her man to come home for his tea
will wait till the paint disintegrates
and ruined dykes admit the esurient sea;
yet this is life too, and the cracked
outhouse door a verifiable fact
as vividly mnemonic as the sunlit
railings that front the houses opposite.

I lived there as a boy and know the coal
glittering in its shed, late-afternoon
lambency informing the deal table,
the ceiling cradled in a radiant spoon.

I must be lying low in a room there,
a strange child with a taste for verse,
while my hard-nosed companions dream of war
on parched veldt and fields of rainswept gorse.

Derry Morning

The mist clears and the cavities
glow black in the rubbled city's
broken mouth. An early crone,
muse of a fitful revolution
wasted by the fray, she sees
her *aisling* falter in the breeze,
her oak-grove vision hesitate
by empty dock and city gate.

Here it began, and here at last
it fades into the finite past
or seems to: clattering shadows whop
mechanically over pub and shop.
A strangely pastoral silence rules
the shining roofs and murmuring schools;
for this is how the centuries work —
two steps forward, one step back.

Hard to believe this tranquil place,
its desolation almost peace,
was recently a boom town wild
with expectation, each unscheduled
incident a measurable
tremor on the Richter Scale
of world events, each vibrant scene
translated to the drizzling screen.

What of the change envisioned here,
the quantum leap from fear to fire?
Smoke from a thousand chimneys strains
one way beneath the returning rains
that shroud the bomb-sites, while the fog
of time receives the ideologue.
A Russian freighter bound for home
mourns to the city in its gloom.

Rock Music

The ocean glittered quietly in the moonlight
while heavy metal rocked the discothèques;
space-age Hondas gurgled half the night,
fired by the prospect of fortuitous sex.
I sat late at the window, blind with rage,
and listened to the tumult down below,
trying to concentrate on the printed page
as if such obsolete bumph could save us now.

(Frank Ifield, Helen Shapiro, where are you now?
Every night by the window here I sit.
Sandie and Bobby, I remember you —
as for the Arcadia, though I remember it,
it no longer remembers the uncouth Coke-heads
who trembled here in nineteen fifty-six
in ice-cream parlours and amusement arcades;
oddities all, we knew none of the tricks.

Cinema organ, easy listening, swing, doowop, bebop,
sedate me with your subliminal sublime
and give me that old trashy fifties pop,
suburban burblings of an earlier time;
the boogie bins bouncing in rotary light,
give me my toxic shame, mean woman blues,
that old self-pity where, lonesome tonight,
I sit here snarling in my blue suede shoes.)

Next morning, wandering on the strand, I heard
left-over echoes of the night before
dwindle to echoes, and a single bird
drown with a whistle that residual roar.
Rock music started up on every side —
whisper of algae, click of stone on stone,
a thousand limpets left by the ebb tide
unanimous in their silent inquisition.

Everything Is Going to Be All Right

How should I not be glad to contemplate
the clouds clearing beyond the dormer window
and a high tide reflected on the ceiling?
There will be dying, there will be dying,
but there is no need to go into that.
The lines flow from the hand unbidden
and the hidden source is the watchful heart;
the sun rises in spite of everything
and the far cities are beautiful and bright.
I lie here in a riot of sunlight
watching the day break and the clouds flying.
Everything is going to be all right.

Tractatus

'The world is everything that is the case'
from the fly giving up in the coal shed
to the Winged Victory of Samothrace.
Give blame, praise, to the fumbling God
who hides, shame-facèdly, His agèd face;
whose light retires behind its veil of cloud.

The world, though, is also so much more —
everything that is the case imaginatively.
Tacitus believed mariners could *hear*
the sun sinking into the western sea;
and who would question that titanic roar,
the steam rising wherever the edge may be?

A Garage in Co. Cork

Surely you paused at this roadside oasis
in your nomadic youth, and saw the mound
of never-used cement, the curious faces,
the soft-drink ads and the uneven ground
rainbowed with oily puddles, where a snail
had scrawled its pearly, phosphorescent trail.

Like a frontier store-front in an old western
it might have nothing behind it but thin air,
building materials, fruit boxes, scrap iron,
dust-laden shrubs and coils of rusty wire,
a cabbage white fluttering in the sodden
silence of an untended kitchen garden —

Nirvana! But the cracked panes reveal a dark
interior echoing with the cries of children.
Here in this quiet corner of Co. Cork
a family ate, slept, and watched the rain
dance clean and cobalt the exhausted grit
so that the mind shrank from the glare of it.

Where did they go? South Boston? Cricklewood?
Somebody somewhere thinks of this as home,
remembering the old pumps where they stood,
antique now, squirting juice into a cream
Lagonda or a dung-caked tractor while
a cloud swam on a cloud-reflecting tile.

Surely a whitewashed suntrap at the back
gave way to hens, wild thyme, and the first few
shadowy yards of an overgrown cart track,
tyres in the branches such as Noah knew —
beyond, a swoop of mountain where you heard,
disconsolate in the haze, a single blackbird.

Left to itself, the functional will cast
a deathbed glow of picturesque abandon.
The intact antiquities of the recent past,
dropped from the retail catalogues, return
to the materials that gave rise to them
and shine with a late sacramental gleam.

A god who spent the night here once rewarded
natural courtesy with eternal life —
changing to petrol pumps, that they be spared
for ever there, an old man and his wife.
The virgin who escaped his dark design
sanctions the townland from her prickly shrine.

We might be anywhere but are in one place only,
one of the milestones of Earth residence
unique in each particular, the thinly
peopled hinterland serenely tense —
not in the hope of a resplendent future
but with a sure sense of its intrinsic nature.

The Woods

Two years we spent
down there, in a quaint
outbuilding bright with recent paint.

A green retreat,
secluded and sedate,
part of a once great estate,

it watched our old
banger as it growled
with guests and groceries through heat and cold,

and heard you tocsin
mealtimes with a spoon
while I sat typing in the sun.

Above the yard
an old clock had expired
the night Lenin arrived in Petrograd.

Hapsburgs and Romanovs
had removed their gloves
in the drawing rooms and alcoves

of the manor house;
but these illustrious
ghosts never imposed on us.

Enough that the pond
steamed, the apples ripened,
the chestnuts on the gravel opened.

Ragwort and hemlock,
cinquefoil and ladysmock
throve in the shadows at the back;

beneath the trees
foxgloves and wood anemones
looked up with tearful metamorphic eyes.

We woke the rooks
on narrow, winding walks
familiar from the story books,

or visited
a disused garden shed
where gas masks from the war decayed;

and we knew peace
splintering the thin ice
on the bathtub drinking trough for cows.

But how could we
survive indefinitely
so far from the city and the sea?

Finding, at last,
too creamy for our taste
the fat profusion of that feast,

we carried on
to chaos and confusion,
our birthright and our proper portion.

Another light
than ours convenes the mute
attention of those woods tonight —

while we, released
from that pale paradise,
confront the darkness in another place.

Craigvara House

That was the year
of the black nights and clear
mornings, a mild elation touched with fear;

a watchful anomie,
heart silence, day-long reverie
while the wind made harpstrings on the sea

and the first
rain of winter burst
earthwards as if quenching a great thirst.

A mist of spray
hung over the shore all day
while I slumped there re-reading *La Nausée*

or knocked a coal,
releasing squeaky gas until
it broke and tumbled into its hot hole.

Night fell on a rough
sea, on a moonlit basalt cliff,
huts with commandments painted on the roof,

and rain wept down
the raw slates of the town,
cackling maniacally in pipe and drain.

I slowly came
to treasure my asylum
(a flat with a sea view, the living room

furnished with frayed
chintz, cane chairs and faded
watercolours of Slemish and Torr Head —

no phone, no television,
nothing to break my concentration,
the new-won knowledge of my situation);

and it was there,
choosing my words with care,
I sat down and began to write once more.

When snowflakes
wandered on to the rocks
I thought, home is where the heart breaks —

the lost domain
of weekends in the rain,
the Sunday sundae and the sexual pain.

I stared each night
at a glow of yellow light
over the water where the interned sat tight

and during storms
imagined the clenched farms
'with dreadful faces throng'd and fiery arms'.

Sometime before
spring I found in there
the frequency I had been looking for

and crossed by night
a dark channel, my eyesight
focused upon a flickering pier light.

I slept then and,
waking early, listened
entranced to the pea-whistle sound

of a first thrush
practising on a whin bush
a new air picked up in Marrakesh.

And then your car
parked with a known roar
and you stood smiling at the door —

as if we might
consider a bad night
as over and step out into the sunlight.

The Globe in Carolina

The earth spins to my fingertips and
pauses beneath my outstretched hand;
white water seethes against the green
capes where the continents begin.
Warm breezes move the pines and stir
the hot dust of the piedmont where
night glides inland from town to town.
I love to see that sun go down.

It sets in a coniferous haze
beyond Georgia while the anglepoise
rears like a moon to shed its savage
radiance on the desolate page,
on Dvořák sleeves and Audubon
bird prints; an electronic brain
records the concrete music of
our hardware in the heavens above.

From Hatteras to the Blue Ridge
night spreads like ink on the unhedged
tobacco fields and clucking lakes,
bringing the lights on in the rocks
and swamps, the farms and motor courts,
substantial cities, kitsch resorts —
until, to the mild theoptic eye,
America is its own night sky.

Out in the void and staring hard
at the dim stone where we were reared,
great mother, now the gods have gone
we place our faith in you alone,
inverting the procedures which
knelt us to things beyond our reach.
Drop of the ocean, may your salt
astringency redeem our fault.

Veined marble, if we only knew,
in practice as in theory, true
redemption lies not in the thrust
of action only, but the trust
we place in our peripheral
night garden in the glory hole
of space, a home from home, and what
devotion we can bring to it.

You lie, an ocean to the east,
your limbs composed, your mind at rest,
asleep in a sunrise which will be
your midday when it reaches me;
and what misgivings I might have
about the final value of
our humanism pale before
the mere fact of your being there.

Five miles away a southbound freight
sings its euphoria to the state
and passes on; unfinished work
awaits me in the scented dark.
The halved globe, slowly turning, hugs
its silence, while the lightning bugs
are quiet beneath the open window,
listening to that lonesome whistle blow.

Girls on the Bridge

— Munch, 1901

Audible trout,
notional midges. Beds,
lamplight and crisp linen wait
in the house there for the sedate
limbs and averted heads
of the girls out

late on the bridge.
The dusty road that slopes
past is perhaps the high road south,
a symbol of world-wondering youth,
of adolescent hopes
and privileges;

but stops to find
the girls content to gaze
at the unplumbed, reflective lake,
their quiet conversational quack
expressive of calm days
and peace of mind.

Grave daughters
of time, you lightly toss
your hair as the long shadows grow
and night begins to fall. Although
your laughter calls across
the dark waters,

a ghastly sun
watches in pale dismay.
Oh you may laugh, being as you are
fair sisters of the evening star,
but wait — if not today
a day will dawn

when the bad dreams
you scarcely know will scatter
the punctual increment of your lives.
The road resumes, and where it curves,
a mile from where you chatter,
somebody screams.

Beyond the Pale

I lie and imagine a first light gleam in the bay
    after one more night of erosion and nearer the grave,
then stand and gaze from the window at break of day
    as a shearwater skims the ridge of an incoming wave;
and I think of my son a dolphin in the Aegean,
    a sprite among sails knife-bright in a seasonal wind,
and wish he were here where currachs walk on the ocean
    to ease with his talk the solitude locked in my mind.

I sit on a stone after noon and consider the glow
    of the sun through mist, a pearl bulb containèdly fierce;
a rain shower darkens the schist for a minute or so,
    then it drifts away and the sloe-black patches disperse.
Croagh Patrick towers like Naxos over the water
    and I think of my daughter at work on her difficult art
and wish she were with me now between thrush and plover,
    wild thyme and sea-thrift, to lift the weight from my heart.

The young sit smoking and laughing on the bridge at evening
    like birds on a telephone pole or notes on a score.
A tin whistle squeals in the parlour, once more it is raining,
    turfsmoke inclines and a wind whines under the door;
and I lie and imagine the lights going on in the harbour
    of white-housed Náousa, your clear definition at night,
and wish you were here to upstage my disconsolate labour
    as I glance through a few thin pages and switch off the light.

Antarctica

(for Richard Ryan)

'I am just going outside and may be some time.'
The others nod, pretending not to know.
At the heart of the ridiculous, the sublime.

He leaves them reading and begins to climb,
goading his ghost into the howling snow;
he is just going outside and may be some time.

The tent recedes beneath its crust of grime
and frostbite is replaced by vertigo:
at the heart of the ridiculous, the sublime.

Need we consider it some sort of crime,
this numb self-sacrifice of the weakest? No,
he is just going outside and may be some time —

in fact, for ever. Solitary enzyme,
though the night yield no glimmer there will glow,
at the heart of the ridiculous, the sublime.

He takes leave of the earthly pantomime
quietly, knowing it is time to go.
'I am just going outside and may be some time.'
At the heart of the ridiculous, the sublime.

Kinsale

The kind of rain we knew is a thing of the past —
deep-delving, dark, deliberate you would say,
browsing on spire and bogland; but today
our sky-blue slates are steaming in the sun,
our yachts tinkling and dancing in the bay
like racehorses. We contemplate at last
shining windows, a future forbidden to no one.

Dawn at St Patrick's

(for Terence Brown)

There is an old
statue in the courtyard
that weeps, like Niobe, its sorrow in stone.
The griefs of the ages she has made her own.
Her eyes are rain-washed but not hard,
her body is covered in mould,
the garden overgrown.

One by one
the first lights come on,
those that haven't been on all night.
Christmas, the harshly festive, has come and gone.
No snow, but the rain pours down
in the first hour before dawn,
before daylight.

Swift's home
for 'fools and mad' has become
the administrative block. Much there
has remained unchanged for many a long year —
stairs, chairs, Georgian windows shafting light and dust,
radiantly white the marble bust
of the satirist;

but the real
hospital is a cheerful
modern extension at the back
hung with restful reproductions of Klee, Dufy and Braque.
Television, Russian fiction, snooker with the staff,
a snifter of Lucozade, a paragraph
of *Newsweek* or the *Daily Mail*

are my daily routine
during the festive season.
They don't lock the razors here
as in Bowditch Hall. We have remained upright —
though, to be frank, the Christmas dinner scene,
with grown men in their festive gear,
was a sobering sight.

I watch the last
planes of the year go past,
silently climbing a cloud-lit sky.
Earthbound, soon I'll be taking a train to Cork
and trying to get back to work
at my sea-lit, fort-view desk
in the turf-smoky dusk.

Meanwhile,
next door, a visiting priest
intones to a faithful dormitory.
I sit on my Protestant bed, a make-believe existentialist,
and stare at the clouds of unknowing. We style,
as best we may, our private destiny;
or so it seems to me

as I chew my thumb
and try to figure out
what brought me to my present state —
an 'educated man', a man of consequence, no bum
but one who has hardly grasped what life is about,
if anything. My children, far away,
don't know where I am today,

in a Dublin asylum
with a paper whistle and a mince pie,
my bits and pieces making a home from home.
I pray to the rain clouds that they never come
where their lost father lies, that their mother thrives
    and that I
may measure up to them
before I die.

Soon a new year
will be here demanding, as before,
modest proposals, resolute resolutions, a new leaf,
new leaves. This is the story of my life,
the story of all lives everywhere,
mad fools wherever we are,
in here or out there.

Light and sane
I shall walk down to the train,
into that world whose sanity we know,
like Swift, to be a fiction and a show.
The clouds part, the rain ceases, the sun
casts now upon everyone
its ancient shadow.

from *New York Time*

Sometimes, from beyond the skyscrapers, the cry of a tugboat
finds you in your insomnia, and you remember this desert of
iron and cement is an island.
                        — Albert Camus, *American Journals*

Winter; a short walk from the 10th St. pier —
and what of the kick-start that should be here?
The fishy ice lies thick on Gansevoort
around the corner, and the snow shines bright
about your country house this morning. Short
the time left to find the serenity
which for a lifetime has eluded me . . .
A rented 'studio apartment' in New York
five blocks from the river, time to think and work,
long-suffering friends and visitors, the bars
where Dylan Thomas spent his final hours,
God rest him; but there's something missing here
in this autistic slammer, some restorative
laid like a magic wand on everything —
on bed, chair, desk and air conditioner.
I often visualize in the neon slush
that great heartbreaking moment in *The Gold Rush*
where Chaplin, left alone on New Year's Eve,
listens to life's feast from his little shack
and the strains of 'Auld Lang Syne' across the snow.
Oh, show me how to recover my lost nerve!
The radiators knock, whistle and sing.
I toss and turn and listen, when I wake,
to the first bird and the first garbage truck,
seeing the 'lordly' Hudson 'hardly' flow
to New York Harbour and the sea below.

The lights go out along the Jersey shore
and, as Manhattan faces east once more,
dawn's early light on bridge and water tower,
Respighi's temperate nightingale on WQXR
pipes up though stronger stations throng the air —
a radio serendipity to illustrate
the resilience of our lyric appetite,
carnivalesque or studiously apart,
on tap in offices, lofts and desperate 'hoods
to Lorca's 'urinating multitudes'
while I make tea and wait for the ghastly news
at eight; but first the nightingale. Sing, Muse.

Somewhere along Route 1 — Plantation, Tavernier —
cloud-splitting Angie broke over the Keys last year
in June, the earliest ever, bringing torrential rains,
though it wasn't one of those really *terrible* hurricanes
you hear about, that wreck towns and wreak atrocities
on isolated farms, snug harbours, close communities,
but a swift cloud-stream of premonitory showers
that waltzed off in the direction of New Orleans
irrigating pine and cedar, lemon groves and sandbars
while the Bahamas heaved in still turbulent seas.
The outskirts of Key West, when we got there,
you driving, a white bandana in your hair
and Satchmo growling from the car radio,
were still where they were supposed to be and, calm
between downpours, red poinciana, jasmine, palm
and the white frame houses built a century ago
by tough skippers against cyclone and tornado.
The town gasped in a tropical heatwave
and I recalled old Mr Temple's narrative
in *Key Largo*, the great nameless storm of 1935
that killed 800 people, it did too, and blew
the East Coast Railroad into the ocean — true,
the bridges are still standing, but that was the last train.
Suave mari magno turbantibus aequora ventis
e terra magnum alterius spectare laborem:
it's cool, when gale-force winds trouble the waters,
to watch from shore the tribulations of others.

　　Uh-oh, before dawn it came round again,
fat drops hitting on storm lanterns, demented budgies
screeching beyond the pool and the churning trees;
and I pictured the vast turmoil undersea,
a mute universe of sponge and anemone,

of conch and snapper, octopus and algae,
odd fish of every stripe in their coral conservatories,
while counting the chimes of St Mary's, Star of the Sea.
Later, exhausted hens on the telephone lines,
dishevelled dogs in the flooded Bahamian lanes:
chaos, *triste tropique* — till, mauve and rose,
flecked with pistachio cloud, a new kind of day arose
and I saw why once to these shores came other cold
solitaries down from the north in search of love and poetry
to sing in the crashing, galaxy-lit sea porches.
It was one of those far-out, raw mornings, the beaches
strewn with wrack, and a derelict dawn moon,
mountains and craters in visible cameo, yearned
close to the earth as if murmuring to return —
a wreckers' morning, with everyone a bit lost
as if landed from Senegal or the Ivory Coast.

Why so soon in the season? Radio and TV
spoke of 'El Niño', the fabulous, hot tide-thrust
born in December off Peru like the infant Christ
sea-changing *all* with its rough magic; and advised
of hurricanes to come, so that one feared not only
for Cuban cabin and gimcrack condominium
but for the 'sleek and effortless vacation home'
featured in the current issue of *Key Design*,
the 'storm-resistant' dream house with its 'vinyl membrane',
a bait fridge and 'teak tarpon-fighting chair';
for roads and bridges, lighthouses, any structure
presumed permanent; towns and cities everywhere
vulnerable to a trickle of sand, to a breath of fresh air;
and thought of the fragility of all architecture,
the provisional nature even of aerospace.
I keep on my desk here a coarse handful of Florida sea gorse
and remember, this wintry night, that summery place —
how we strolled out there on the still quaking docks

shaken but exhilarated, turned to retrace
our steps up Caroline St., and sat in Pepe's
drinking rum and Coke with retired hippies
who long ago gave up on the land and settled among the rocks.

17 ST BRIDGET'S DAY

A roof over my head, protected from the rain,
I'm reading, pilgrim father, your letters to your son
and wondering if, unlike you, I should head for home.
Escaping the turbulence of this modern Rome
in a flurry of skyline views and exploding foam,
I can see that 747 in flight over Nova Scotia,
Lahinch and Limerick, snoring back to the future;
I can see the old stormy island from the air,
its meteorological gaiety and despair,
some evidence of light industry and agriculture,
familiar contours, turfsmoke on field and town;
I can even hear the cabin crew's soft '*fáilte*'
and the strains of 'My Lagan Love' as we touch down.
A recovering Ulster Protestant from Co. Down,
I'll walk the Dublin lanes as the days grow shorter,
I who once had poems in *The New Yorker*,
and spend old age, if any, in an old mac
with the young audibly sneering behind my back,
deafened by seagulls and the playground cries
of children — ourselves, once — by perilous seas.
Now, listening to the *rus-in-urbe*, spring-in-winter noise
of late-night diners while the temperatures rise
and the terrible wind-chill factor abates, I realize
the daffodils must be out in ditch and glen
and windows soon flung wide to the spring rain;
and marvel how, a figure out of the past,
an old man in a hurry, you stuck it here to the last,
negotiating the icefields of 8th Avenue
to die on West 29th of the 'Asian' flu.

But first you met by chance at the riverside
a young woman with a sick child she tried to hide
(not out of shame, you felt, but anguished pride),

soft-spoken, 'from Donnybrook', amid the alien corn.
'It pained me that her bright image should fade.'
Thus your epiphany, and you wrote to explain:
'The nightingale sings with its breast against a thorn,
it's out of pain that personality is born.'
Things you understood: children, the human face,
'something finer than honesty', the kindness
of women and the priority of the real.
Things that puzzled you: economy, fear,
the argument from design, the need to feel secure,
the belief in another world besides this one here.
Despite your rationalism, did it ever appear
that the universe might be *really* 'magical', sir,
and you yourself a showing-forth of that soul?
'Art is dreamland.' When you rejoined the whole
what glimpse was given to you in the black hole?
Now, to 'Yeats, Artist and Writer', may we add
that you were at home here and in human nature
but also, in your own words, lived and died
like all of us, then as now, 'an exile and a stranger'?

18 RAIN

Once upon a time it was let me out and let me go —
the night flight over deserts, amid cloud,
a dream of discipline and fit solitude.
Now, drifters, loners, harsh and disconsolate,
'inane and unappeased', we come knocking late;
and now it's take me back and take me in.
So take us in where we set out long ago,
the enchanted garden in the lost domain,
the vigilant lamplight glimpsed through teeming rain,
the house, the stove in the kitchen, the warm bed,
the hearth, *vrai lieu*, ranged crockery overhead,
'felicitous space' lost to the tribes. I lodge
one window slightly open to let in the night air
— ten below, these nights, on average —
heating the street, the clouds, the stratosphere,
and peer down through the fire escape. It's broad
day all night on the 24-hour film-set,
kliegs bright on stadium and construction site;
but a civilization based on superfluous light
concedes no decent dark, so we create
with blinds and blankets our own private night
to keep the glare out. Searchlights and dead stars
pick out the Trump Tower and the United Nations,
the halls of finance, the subway walls of the brain,
the good, the bad, the ugly and the insane,
the docks and Governor's Island; and the bars
where the lost and the disappointed feel no pain
are empty except for the all-night populations,
no homes to go to but their eternal one.
This is the hour of the chained door and the locked gate,
harsh blues of the rowdy and the unfortunate,
and the fetishes are wakeful in their places —
lamp, chair, desk, oil-heater and bookcases

brisk with a bristling, mute facticity
connecting them to the greater community
of wood and minerals throughout the city.
When the present occupant is no longer here
and durables prove transient, as they do,
all will survive somehow; the pictures too,
prints, posters, reproductions, such as they are:
the obvious sea-born, shell-borne Aphrodite,
Dunluce, 'The Doors of Dublin', Whitman in a suit,
Monet skiffs on the Seine, a window by Bonnard,
Leech's convent garden, a Hopper light,
Hokusai's wave, Lichtenstein's *ingénue*
shedding a tear ('But, Brad . . .') beside the door
and (look!) my favourite, over there on the right,
picked up at a yard sale in Connecticut,
Kroyer's *Women on the Beach*, a hazy shore,
their footprints in the sand to the waterline,
the human presence since we live here too —
all primal images in their different ways
watching for springtime and the lengthening days.

   Jequirity, monkshood, nightshade, celandine.
The friends and contemporaries begin to go
— Nina Gilliam, Eugene Lambe, and others too.
'A dry soul is best'; and at night to lie
empty of mind, the heart at peace; *and thou,*
dark mother, cave of wonders, open now
to our languor the interior of the rose
that closes round volition, and disclose
your secret, be it Byzantium or the sphere
all centre, no circumference . . . I pretend
you're here beside me; guardian angel, best friend,
practitioner of tough love and conservation,
I'd say make all safe and harmonious in the end
did I not know the voyage is never done

for, even as we speak, somewhere a plane
gains altitude in the moon's exilic glare
or a car slips into gear in a silent lane . . .
I think of the homeless, no rm. at the inn;
far off, the gaseous planets where they spin,
the starlit towers of Nineveh and Babylon,
the secret voice of nightingale and dolphin,
fish crowding the Verrazano Bridge; and see,
even in the icy heart of February,
crocus and primrose. When does the thaw begin?
We have been too long in the cold. — Take us in; take us in!

from *Decadence*

2 AXEL'S CASTLE

A mature artist takes the material closest to hand.
— George Moore

Rain all day, now clouds clear; a brief sun, the winds die.
A wan streak of bilious light in the sky before dark,
'the attic study and the unfinished work'.
Only at dusk Athene's owl will fly,
only at dusk does wisdom return to the park.
On winter evenings, as the cars flash by,
what hides there in the kingdom of mould and bark?
Beyond the iron railings and the little gate
perhaps a fox stirs, and dead leaves conflate
in a dried-up fountain crisp-packet and matchbox,
the bright pavilion silent in its nook;
dead leaves up here too, lamplight night and day.
Commuters hustle home to Terenure and Foxrock
while I sit in the inner city with my book
— *Fanny Hill, À Rebours, The Picture of Dorian Gray* —
the pleasures of the text, periphrasis and paradox,
some languorous prose at odds with phone and fax.
The psychiatrist locks up and puts out the light
on desk and couch in his consulting rooms.
It's cold up here in the city of litter and drums
while fires glow in the hearths of suburban homes.
I have no peacocks, porphyries, prie-dieux,
no lilies, cephalotis, nepenthes, 'unnatural' vices,
yet I too toil not neither do I spin, I too
have my carefully constructed artificial paradises.
A foxy lady slips into her shoes
and leaves me words of wisdom; when she goes
I sit here like Domitian in a hecatomb of dead flies,
an armchair explorer in an era of cheap flight
diverted by posters, steamer and seaplane

at rest in tropical ports. I read where your man
transforms his kitchen into a quarterdeck
to simulate ocean travel and not get sick.
I get sea breezes in my own galley all right,
particularly before dawn when, war in heaven, I hear
remote winds rippling in the stratosphere
and regret never having visited Rio, Shanghai,
Haiti, Kyōto or the South Seas; though why
travel when imagination can get you there in a tick
and you're not plagued by the package crowd? A mature
artist takes the material closest to hand;
besides, in our post-modern world economy
one tourist site is much like another site
and the holy city comes down to a Zeno tour,
the closer you get the more it recedes from sight
and the more morons block your vision.
                                        Beyond
the backlit tree-tops of Fitzwilliam Square
a high window is showing one studious light,
somebody sitting late at a desk like me.
There are some diehards still on the upper floors,
a Byzantine privacy in mews and lane,
but mostly now the famous Georgian doors
will house a junk-film outfit or an advertising agency.
The fountain's flute is silent though time spares
the old beeches with their shades of Coole demesne;
inward investment conspires against old decency,
computer talks to computer, machine to answering machine.

We stand — not many of us — in a new cemetery
on a cold hillside in Co. Down, your few
last friends and relatives, declining too,
and stare at an open grave or out to sea,
the lough half hidden by great drifts of rain.
Only a few months since you were snug at home
in a bungalow glow, keeping provincial time
in the chimney corner, *News-Letter* and *Woman's Own*
on your knee, wool-gathering by Plato's firelight,
a grudging flicker of flame on anthracite.
Inactive since your husband died, your chief
concern the 'appearances' that ruled your life
in a neighbourhood of bay windows and stiff
gardens shivering in the salt sea air,
the sunburst ideogram on door and gate,
you knew the secret history of needlework,
bread-bin and laundry basket awash with light.
The figure in the *Republic* returns to the cave,
a Dutch interior where cloud shadows move,
to examine the intimate spaces, chest and drawer,
the lavender in the linen, the savings book,
the kitchen table silent with nobody there.
Shall we say the patience of an angel? No,
not unless angels be thought anxious too.
God knows you had reason to be; and yet
with your wise monkeys and 'Dresden' figurines,
your junk chinoiserie and coy pastoral scenes,
you too were an artist, a rage-for-order freak
setting against a man's aesthetic of cars and golf
your ornaments and other breakable stuff.
Just visible from your window the 6th-century
abbey church of Columbanus and Malachi,
'light of the world' once in the monastic ages,

home of antiphonary and the golden pages
of radiant scripture; though you had your own
idea of the beautiful, not unrelated to Tolstoy
but formed in a tough city of ships and linen,
Harland & Wolff, Mackie's, Gallaher's, Lyle & Kinahan
and your own York St. Flax Spinning Co. Ltd.;
daft musicals at the Curzon and the Savoy.

    Beneath a Castilian sky, at a great mystic's rococo tomb,
I thought of the plain Protestant fatalism of home.
Remember 1690; prepare to meet thy God —
I grew up among washing lines and grey skies,
pictures of Brookeborough on the gable ends,
revolvers, RUC, 'B' Specials, law-'n'-order,
a hum of drums above the summer glens
shattering the twilight over lough water
in a violent post-industrial sunset blaze
while you innocently hummed 'South of the Border',
'On a Slow Boat to China', 'Beyond the Blue Horizon'.
Little soul, the body's guest and companion,
this is a cold epitaph from your only son,
the wish genuine if the tone ambiguous.
Oh, I can love you now that you're dead and gone
to the many mansions in your mother's house;
all artifice stripped away, we give you back to nature
but something of you, perhaps the incurable ache
of art, goes with me as I travel south
past misty drumlins, shining lanes to the shore,
above the Mournes a final helicopter,
sun-showers and rainbows all the way through Louth,
cottages buried deep in ivy and rhododendron,
ranch houses, dusty palms, blue skies of the republic . . .

Ghosts

We live the lives our parents never knew
when they sang 'Come Back to Sorrento'.
Driving west in the evening from Pompeii,
its little houses sealed up in a tomb
of ash and pumice centuries ago
and now exposed to the clear light of day,
we found an old hotel with a sea view
and Naples' lights reflected in the bay
where, with a squeal of seagulls far below,
white curtains blew like ghosts into the room.

Roman Script

Nei rifiuti del mondo nasce un nuovo mondo.
— Pasolini

I

Rain in the night; now cock-crow and engine hum
wake us at first light on the Janiculum
and we open the shutters to extravagant mists
behind which an autumn sun hotly insists:
parasol pine, low dove and glistening drop,
bright lemon, jonquil, jasmine and heliotrope —
the Respighi moment, life mimicking art again
as when the fiddles provoke line-dancing rain.

2

Turn back into the room where sunlight shows
dim ceilings, domino tiles, baroque frescoes,
a scenic interior, a theatrical space
for Byronic masquerade or Goldoni farce,
vapours and swordsmanship, the cape and fan,
the amorous bad-boy and the glamorous nun,
boudoir philosophy, night music on balconies,
the gondola section nodding as in a sea breeze.

3

Rome of conspiracy theories and lost causes,
exiles have died here in your haunted palaces
where our own princes, flushed with wine and hope,
they say, and the squeal of a lone bagpipe
torn from the wild and windy western ocean,
dreamed up elaborate schemes of restoration —

a world more distant now than Pompeian times
with the shipyards visible from the nymphaeums.

4

Type up the new stuff, nap between four and five
when for a second time you come alive
with flies that linger in November light
and moths not even camphor puts to flight;
listen with them to sepia furniture
and piano practice from the flat next door;
watch where the poplar spires of evening thin
to smoke-stains on the ochreous travertine.

5

Now out you go among the *botteghe oscure*
and fluttering street lamps of Trastevere,
over the bridge where Fiat and Maserati
burn up the racetrack of the eternal city,
floodlit naiad and triton; for at this hour
the beautiful and damned are in Harry's Bar
or setting out for pit stops, sexy dives
and parties, as in the movie of our lives.

6

Here they are, Nero, Julia, Poppaea, Diocletian
and the shrewd popes of a later dispensation
at ease in bath-house and in Coliseum
or raping young ones in the venial gym —
as the prophet said, as good a place as any

to watch the end of the world; to watch, at least,
the late mutation of the romantic egotist
when the knock comes at last for Don Giovanni.

7

Snap out of your art fatigue and take a trip
to church and basilica, forum, fountain and frieze,
to the Sistine Chapel's violent comic strip
or the soft marble thighs of Persephone; seize
real presence, the art-historical sublime,
in an intricate owl-blink Nikon moment of time,
in a flash-photography lightning storm above
Cecilia's actual body, Endymion's actual grave.

8

Mid-morning noise of prisoners playing hard
in the Regina Coeli's echoing exercise yard —
for even the wretched of the earth are here
with instructions to entertain the visitor;
and we walk in reality, framed as virtuality,
as in a film set, Cinecittà, a cinema city
where life is a waking dream in broad daylight
and everything is scripted for our delight.

9

Others were here, *comunque*, who dreamed in youth
of a society based on hope and faith —
the poet of internment, solitude, morning sea,
of the lost years when we used to fall in love

not with women themselves but some commodity,
a hat, a pair of shoes, a blouse, a glove
(to him death came with the eyes of a new age,
a facile cynicism restyled as image);

10

and the poet of poverty, ash on the night wind,
starlight and tower blocks on waste ground,
peripheral rubbish dumps beyond the noise
of a circus, where sedated girls and boys
put out for a few bob on some building site
in the cloudy imperium of ancient night
and in the ruins, amid disconsolate lives
on the edge of the artful city, a myth survives.

11

His is the true direction we have lost
since his corpse showed up on the beach at Ostia
and life as we know it evolved into imagery,
production values and revised history,
the genocidal corporate imperative
and the bright garbage on the incoming wave
best seen at morning rush hour in driving rain:
'in the refuse of the world a new world is born'.

Shapes and Shadows

— William Scott, oil on canvas,
Ulster Museum

The kitchens would grow bright
in blue frames; outside, still
harbour and silent cottages
from a time of shortages,
shapes deft and tranquil,
black kettle and black pot.

Too much the known structures
those simple manufactures,
communion of frying pans,
skinny beans and spoons,
colander and fish slice
in a polished interior space.

But tension of hand and heart
abstracted the growing art
to a dissonant design
and a rich dream of paint,
on the grim basic plan
a varied white pigment

knifed and scrubbed, in one
corner an enigmatic
study in mahogany;
beige-biscuit left; right
a fat patch of white,
bread and milk in agony.

Rough brushwork here, thick
but vague; for already
behind these there loom
shades of the prehistoric,

ghosts of colour and form,
furniture, function, body —

as if to anounce the death
of preconception and myth
and start again on the fresh
first morning of the world
with snow, ash, whitewash,
limestone, mother-of-pearl,

bleach, paper, soap, foam
and cold kitchen cream,
to find in the nitty-gritty
of surfaces and utensils
the shadow of a presence,
a long-sought community.

Lapis Lazuli

(for Harry Clifton)

A whole night sky that serves as a paperweight,
a chunk of rock as if fallen from space
sits shimmering on the desk, an azure piece
of planet, veined with gold and white,
uncut and knobbly as a meteorite.
Even with no twinkly sages on the stone
it radiates hard wisdom of its own.

Night-fashioned in moonstruck Afghanistan
this sulphurous lump, a 'complex silicate',
ethereal blue beloved of god and man,
speaks authenticity these doubtful days
of lazy cloud and random haze —
days speculative as watching paint dry,
while Buddha and a Yeats head supervise.

I look each morning for that dense astronomy
and at noon blind to its dark myths.
An ember glowing from its grate,
the real thing in its natural state,
we seek the glimmer of those secret depths,
the key to that mysterious heart.
With lapis lazuli what need for art?

The Widow of Kinsale

Cionn tSáile, 'Head of the Tide',
knew me once as a young bride
but those days are gone;
a rock exposed to the sun,
sardonic, cold and stiff,
I go with the ebb of life.

The salt surge in my veins
whispers its age and drains
down to the shrinking sea:
no more high tide for me.
Stylish I was and not
got up in this old coat.

Young ones now think only
of fashion and easy money —
as we did once, except
we never had much of it:
real people were the thing,
to hear them talk and sing.

When I was a girl we thought
more highly of our admirers.
I opened my young body
gravely to their desires;
now I am an old lady,
unwanted and unsought.

War widow and sea widow
many years on the shelf,
I've better things to do
than my once sexy self,
my beauty and high tone
nothing but skin and bone.

I was a fierce temptation
to wild, generous men
of my own generation;
lovingly I would watch
while driving them insane.
Now look at this eyepatch.

Once a wife and mother
beset by childish squabbles,
I live alone with a plethora
of stuff in the loud fridge:
plaice, chops and vegetables,
enough for a new ice age.

I who was bright and gay
in the wine-and-roses years
am briskly polite today
to gossipy old neighbours;
my white head in the clouds,
I avoid the holiday crowds.

Crows croak from the convent
where once we used to skip.
Everything has been taken
since it is not convenient —
the upper windows broken,
the lower ones boarded up.

Sometimes I drive over
in my olive vintage Rover
to Bantry or even Dingle
and think of the times I knew
when everyone was single;
but now they are so few

that mostly I prefer
a comfortable armchair.
I could re-read for ever
the novels of William Trevor,
that lovely man, and watch
starlight in the dark porch.

Calm and alone at last,
I wake up in the night.
A superstitious atheist,
I now befriend the clergy
and go to church despite
the new revised liturgy;

but my true guiding spirit
is something I inherit,
a thing dim and opaque,
a lighthouse in the fog,
a lamp hung in a wood
to light my solitude,

breastplate and consolation
whatever the situation:
increasing aches and pains,
the silence in the womb
as the life force wanes,
my children far from home.

Peewits run on the strand
as evening light warms
primitive life forms,
islands of shining sand,
and the ebb tide withdraws
with a chuckle of bony claws.

Calypso

I

Homer was wrong, she never 'ceased to please'.
Once he'd escaped from Circe's magic castle,
the toxic cup, shape-shifting witcheries;
from the underworld, from Aeolus' watery roar,
the high-pitched Sirens' penetrating whistle,
cliff monsters, divine anger, broken boats,
on soft, tinkling shingle he crept ashore
through juniper and parsley, cows and goats,
and found the hot path to her open door,
a cart parked in the lane, a smoking fire.

Gaily distracting him from his chief design
she welcomed him with open arms and thighs,
teaching alternatives to war and power.
A wild girl rushing to the head like wine,
she held him closely with her braided coils,
her swift insistence, aromatic oils,
her mild, beguiling glance, tuning his days
to a slow sea rhythm; and through a salty haze
he watched her moving as in a golden shower
or swimming with her nymphs from the seashore.

Red sails in the sunset where the dripping prows
rapped out a drum rhythm on uncertain seas
of skimming birds, a lonely pine or shrine —
but the sea's secrets diminished on dry land,
darker than they could know or understand,
and vanished in a blink, night coming on
wherever they put ashore to rest. A whorled
conch whispered about a recent, far-off world
with oars sunk in sand marking the graves
of those lost to chance or vindictive waves.

Some harsh, some murderous with savage gulls
squatting in triumph amid scattered skulls
buzzing with flies, he knew unfortunate isles,
the eternal conflict between sea and stone,
the palpitating heat of the noon sun.
He prayed for an end to these moronic wars,
burned wasteful sacrifices to the vague stars
and dreamed of honey, yoghurt, figs and wine
on night beaches far from the life he knew,
silent, unlit; but a faint murmur, a faint glow.

Those were the times he thought about his wife,
remembering their lives in a former life,
her handsome profile, her adventurous heart
and proud posture. At sea and lost he wept
for jokes and music, promises unkept,
sandals on board and tile, shared places, friends,
shared history, origins, those woods and glens,
his brisk departure from the family hearth
a conscious risk; but nature took its course
leaving him desolation and long remorse.

2

Ithaca, 'home', not far now as the kite flew,
he sniffed those evenings when a sea wind blew
but lingered in that cave behind the dunes
enchanted now by hazel and sea-grey eyes,
the star-flow of the hair, the skittish tones,
sand-quivering foam, long leisure, lip and gland
in early-morning light, the sun ablaze
through leaves and linen, through her open hand,
briar and cumuli; so the years unwound
to a whisper of spring water and kitchen noise.

Homer was right though about the important thing,
the redemptive power of women; for this narrative,
unlike the blinding shields, is womanly stuff.
The witch bewitches, the owl-winged sisters sing,
some kind girl takes charge within the shadow
of a calm glade where the sea finds a meadow;
much-sought Penelope in her new resolute life
has wasted no time acting the stricken widow
and even the face that sank the final skiff
knows more than beauty; beauty is not enough.

Penelope of course, with the husband gone,
was instantly besieged by plausible men
and the wild rumours now in circulation;
the palace, ruined by competing suitors,
hosted intrigue, conspiracy and confusion,
its shadow crumbling in Ionian waters.
He knew nothing of this; or, if he did,
felt he had no more heart now for a fight,
asking the Pleiades or a drifting cloud
to let these things unravel as best they might.

He spent his days there in a perpetual summer.
Stuck in a rock-cleft like a beachcomber
washed up, high and dry amid luminous spray,
intent on pond life, wildflowers and wind play,
the immense significance of a skittering ant,
a dolphin-leap or a plunging cormorant,
he learned to live at peace with violent nature,
calm under the skies' grumbling cloud furniture
and bored by practical tackle, iron and grease —
an ex-king and the first philosopher in Greece.

Bemused with his straw hat and driftwood stick,
unmoved by the new wars and the new ships,

he died there, fame and vigour in eclipse,
listening to voices echo, decks and crates
creak in the harbour like tectonic plates —
or was he sharp still in his blithe disgrace,
deliberate pilot of his own foggy shipwreck?
Homer was wrong, he never made it back; or,
if he did, spent many a curious night hour
still questioning that strange, oracular face.

Brian Moore's Belfast

(for Gerald Dawe)

The last trams were still running in those days.
Women wore hats and gloves, nylons, fox fur;
raw fissures lingered where incendiaries
demolished Clifton St. in April of '41:
the big band era, dances and commotion,
but the war ended and rain swept once more
parks and playgrounds, chapel and horse trough
'to die in the faraway mists over Belfast Lough'.

Do this, do that, Road Closed, No Entry, Stop! —
a world of signs and yet the real thing too:
even now I catch a whiff of brack and bap,
the soap and ciggies of the *disparus*.
Buns from Stewart's, gobstoppers from Graham's,
our crowd intent on our traditional games,
sectarian puzzlement, a swinging rope,
freezing winters, pristine bicycle frames;

school windows under the Cave Hill, childish faces,
uncles and aunties, pipes and lipstick traces,
epiphanies in sheds and woody places:
how can we not love the first life we knew?
'We can dream only what we know,' he said.
I know the whole length of the Antrim Road
and often dream of Salisbury Avenue;
mysterious Hazelwood, I still think of you.

On Riverside Drive and a California beach
such things revisited him, just out of reach,
just as he left them after Naples, Warsaw,
frozen for ever in the austere post-war
where frequent silence keeps its own integrity
and smoky ghosts of the exhausted city

rustle with phantom life whose time is up.
They queue in Campbell's crowded coffee shop

or wait for a bus at Robb's. I can make out
a clutch of gantries, a white sepulchre
grimly vigilant on its tiny acre,
skirts and shirts mid-20th-century style
in dimly lit arcades, carpets of wet
grain at the quayside where a night boat
churns up the dark and a rapturous old girl
sings 'Now Is the Hour' with her eternal smile.

A Lighthouse in Maine

— Edward Hopper

It might be anywhere, that ivory tower
reached by a country road. Granite and sky,
it faces every which way with an air
of squat omniscience, intensely mild,
a polished Buddha figure warm and dry
beyond vegetation; and the sunny glare
striking its shingled houses is no more
celestial than the hot haze of the world.

Built to shed light but also hoarding light,
it sits there dozing in the afternoon
above the ocean like a ghostly moon
patiently waiting to illuminate.
You make a left beyond the town, a right,
you turn a corner and there, ivory-white,
it shines in modest glory above a bay.
Out you get and walk the rest of the way.

Research

An actual conch
like a human head on its side,
washed up and left here by the ebb tide,
a magical sculpture, perfectly arbitrary,
lies as if dropped from orbit.
Oh, they will launch

research to find
ice in the Sea of Rains,
a first dubious twitch of mud and plants,
signs of life on the other planets,
whispers of inchoate mind
and flickering brains.

Meanwhile on Earth
we've mud, plants, pleasure, pain
and even real lives to be getting on with;
seasons for this and that, the works and days
of many mice and men
as Hesiod says.

Best to ignore
'the great ocean of truth',
the undiscovered seas of outer space,
and research this real unconscious conch on the shore
with its polished, archaic face
and its air of myth.

A Quiet Spot

We tire of cities in the end:
the whirr and blur of it, so long your friend,
grows repetitious and you start to choke
on signage, carbon monoxide, the hard look.
You always knew it would come down
to a dozy seaside town —

not really in the country, no,
but within reach of the countryside,
somewhere alive to season, wind and tide,
far field and wind farm. 'Wrong life,' said Adorno,
'can't be lived rightly.' The right place
is a quiet spot like this

where an expanding river spills,
still trout-rich, from the dewy hills
of Cork, still fertile in a morning mist.
So, do you pause to congratulate yourself
out here at the continental shelf,
far from the hysteria,

on the perfect work-life balancing act
you've found after so many a fugitive year
of travel? If so, let the pause be brief.
Gaia demands your love, the patient earth
your airy sneakers tread expects
humility and care.

It's time now to go back at last
beyond irony and slick depreciation,
past hedge and fencing to a clearer vision,
time to create a future from the past,
tune out the babbling radio waves
and listen to the leaves.

The Thunder Shower

A blink of lightning, then
a rumour, a grumble of white rain
growing in volume, rustling over the ground,
drenching the gravel in a wash of sound.
Drops tap like timpani or shine
like quavers on a line.

It rings on exposed tin,
a suite for water, wind and bin,
plinky Poulenc or strongly groaning Brahms'
rain strings, a whole string section that describes
the very shapes of thought in warm
self-referential vibes

and spreading ripples. Soon
the whispering roar is a recital.
Jostling rain crowds, clamorous and vital,
struggle in runnels through the afternoon.
The rhythm becomes a regular beat;
steam rises, body heat —

and now there's city noise,
bits of recorded pop and rock,
the drums, the strident electronic shock,
a vast polyphony, the dense refrain
of wailing siren, truck and train
and incoherent cries.

All human life is there
in the unconfined, continuous crash
whose slow, diffused implosions gather up
car radios and alarms, the honk and beep,
and tiny voices in a crèche
piercing the muggy air.

Squalor and decadence,
the rackety global-franchise rush,
oil wars and water wars, the diatonic
crescendo of a cascading world economy
are audible in the hectic thrash
of this luxurious cadence.

The voice of Baal explodes,
raging and rumbling round the clouds,
frantic to crush the self-sufficient spaces
and reimpose his failed hegemony
in Canaan before moving on
to other simpler places.

At length the twining chords
run thin, a watery sun shines out,
the deluge slowly ceases, the guttural chant
subsides; a thrush sings, and discordant thirds
diminish like an exhausted concert
on the subdominant.

The angry downpour swarms
growling to far-flung fields and farms.
The drains are still alive with trickling water,
a few last drops drip from a broken gutter;
but the storm that created so much fuss
has lost interest in us.

New Space

Swept and scrubbed, the studio fills
with cut cloth, illustrated books,
materials shaped by polished skills
in a time-honoured fashion, one
that aims for a real thing well done
with real significance. Just look

at how green light and shadow fall
on the interior, jug and bowl,
still life, *nature morte*. The place
itself is a still life restored
to living matter, a new space
whose true life is renewed once more.

A coach house in equestrian days,
it makes one with the vegetable
garden beyond the ceramic glaze
inside and the converted stable
loft where an old record plays
to pram and pine and summer breeze.

It's all the one, the clay, the cloth,
art, music and organic growth
nursing the venerable ideal
of spirit lodged within the real.
Tolstoy, who later disapproved
of opera, plays and novels, loved

doorknobs, utensils, toys and song,
the homespun that the peasants wore —
everything simple, strong and clean,
art that was modest, not a chore;
and rhyming verses, not too long,
that say exactly what they mean.

Though the sun rises in a blaze
these mornings, breaking up the haze,
I'm less in love with the sublime,
more interested in the neat rows
laid out to raise the beans and peas,
rosemary, parsley, sage and thyme.

The weight of a bone-handled knife
signifies more in human life
than our aesthetics ever can;
form follows function. Once again
we look to the still living whole
to heal the heart and cure the soul.

Beached Whale

Snow from the north, hail, and a ruffled gull
rises from cold dunes at break of day
when the shore belongs to the gale,
the frozen algae and the beached whale
fluke-thrashing as she breathes her dying
breaths and gradually subsides
under the great weight of her own insides.

The transatlantic dash was nothing to her,
a fine finback, her notion of a trip
some new dimension, gravity defied,
the dive at dusk through the empyrean
whooping and chuckling in her slick and drip,
stinking and scooping up the fry,
rusty and barnacled like an old steamship.

On moonlit nights her bubbling orifices
dribbled for miles, mysterious and capricious,
where she went spouting, eerie as Moby Dick,
far from the known sea lanes, her whistle and click
distinguishable from Cape Clear to Cape Race;
on a calm day she'd snooze
exposed and ruminant on the sunny surface.

Out of her depth now, her rorqual pleats
ivory fading to grey as the tide retreats,
her brain at rest, with her huge size
she has admirers in her drowsy eyes —
surfers and tourists, children, families
who never saw a whale before;
and the news cameras, RTÉ, Channel 4.

A tired eye closes after so many years,
so much experience, travel, league upon league
of ocean, wild sunrises and sunsets,

tropical storms, long vistas, wind and stars;
and she gives up the ghost
not in the unfathomable dark forest
of sea, but here on the strand at Timoleague.

Pliny thought dolphins beached for love of man,
aspiring to human life. A mighty beast
like this has other reasons (pheromone,
exhaustion, age), yet when she gasps her last
bad breath on the glassy sand she gives
her body to flensing knives
and the flesh falls away in heavy leaves —

source once of lamp oil, glue and candle grease.
Dead of some strange respiratory disease,
reduced to the ribcage of an old wreck,
entrails strewn on mud, the stomach
stripped and the organs — heart, liver
and lights — retrieved for research,
she knows we aim to make a study of her;

to study the cortex, the skin thick and thin,
her ancient knowledge of the seas and rocks
we left to climb up on the burning shore
and still revisit in dreams and sex,
where the soft human paw
has the reflex of an unthinking fin
or a nerve twitching in primordial depths.

At the Butler Arms

No boats this week, too choppy, so we watch
from a spread table beneath
a Charlie Chaplin photograph
who often came here for a holiday;
or we drive over to Finian's Cove to study
the eight-mile stretch

of water between here and Sceilig Mhichíl
where the old anchorites
and monks who chose the place and raised
a church, two chapels and six drystone huts,
survived on dulse and mackerel
out in the haze.

No pleasant woodland there, no grazing deer
such as the others knew
above fly-bubbling salmon streams ashore,
in field and forest beneath oak and yew —
not calm, contemplative ease
but violent seas.

Six hundred years of plainchant and response,
gannet and cormorant; six
centuries of the 'crude bronze crucifix'
in Finian's church, chalice and canticle,
prayer book and reading candle,
thistles, sea campions.

How could you get inside their bony heads?
Wrapped up in mystic mists,
they spent the hours and years
wrestling with the hot flesh in their cold beds,
their backs to Europe and the wars,
talking to ghosts.

What news of the great world, of Gaul and Rome,
Iona and Cappadocia? Some,
but late; prostrate at Easter in the nave
they listened to the whistling wave
and saw the sun sink in an infinite ocean
world of its own.

Strong winds continue, so no trip this time.
Still, it could be predictable to climb
to the immense height and the whole shocking
reach of the Atlantic (with special care
since there's no handrail there).
No going back,

is there, to that wild hush of dedication,
to the solitude, the intense belief,
the last rock of an abandoned civilization
whose dim lights glimmered in a distant age
to illuminate at the edge
a future life.

A Country Kitchen

'Walking into eternity'
along the breathing strand
there's that modality
immediately to hand —
spawn, wrack, far-out sea
and Howth Head beyond.

This is how it begins,
devotion to the real things
of a clean-swept morning:
leaf drip and birdsong,
work sounds, the rich
air of a country kitchen.

We toy with rhythm and rhyme
at a freshly lit hearth;
from under a close blanket
of ground fog the earth
opens up to a cloudstream
westwards in the Atlantic.

The world of simple fact
gleams with water, yields
to the plough. A gull race
follows the working tractor.
Quidditas: the used fields
of Ulster and ancient Greece;

and always the same river,
the oracle and universe
with no circumference,
that infinite resource.
If a thing happens once
it happens once for ever.

Balcony of Europe

(for Aidan and Alannah Higgins)

The dictator's portrait dominated the airport
in those days, the first thing you noticed
after the cold police; his arms, a vivid
fistful of forked lightning, blazed
on the bus station and the road north-east
to the olive hills where the novelist lived.
The kitchen tap gave only a dry cough;
it was pitch black up there with the light off.

Down here at the sea-front forty years later,
on the *paseo*, at the Balcón de Europa bar:
cameras, recorded accordion and guitar.
No shortage now of light or water,
everything so much brighter and better —
old wounds healed, old bones reconstituted;
and a young one in a swimsuit plays
on the shore as she did in ancient days

when she wasn't only a girl but a creature
of myth, a Phoenician king's abducted daughter
with a white bull between her knees,
borne out to a sun-white sea shaking with fear
and exhilaration, far from her shocked sisters,
gripping the horns, clutching the curly hair,
et tremulae sinuantur flamine vestes
('her floaty garments fluttering in the breeze').

Monochrome

The coat an uncle bought you as a girl —
tweed by the look of it, in a fifties style,
your blonde hair unfinicky and natural
lying in short waves round the hidden ears.
You're prematurely wise for eighteen years:
that level gaze, and that reserved smile!

A young idealist, your head in the wind,
before travel, sophistication and party time,
you're still living at home in Portballintrae
with its long winter nights and an extreme
cold that can do strange things to the mind,
reading the Brontës and Daphne du Maurier.

Soon enough you'll be in another town
picking out poets from the library shelves,
speaking in tongues, sporting a black gown
and spending your leisure hours with privileged
young gentlemen far too fond of themselves
where I first met you in another age.

Gowned like Czarinas, twirling parasols, you
and Sibyl stood at a roadside in Boulogne
hitching a lift to Greece; later you shone
on your own local afternoon talk show.
Too long a time in London, then the last
years spent on an obscure Indian quest.

Adored as a student, you never quite got over
the shock and glamour of your first lover.
Enamoured of high style, wounded by each
new manifestation of commercial kitsch,
you boggled at the crude, the daft, the naff
promoted by the genius of modern life . . .

This isn't good enough. I should make a list
of what you fancied: islands, freesia, fresh
strawberries, *broderie anglaise*, Schubert, snow;
the people, Maurice and Sandra, you liked best
and favourite phrases, 'kiddiewinks', 'cut a dash',
'a bit of zing', 'knee-trembler', 'the goat's toe'.

The cloudy backdrop gives you a period air
and sure enough you loved the cloudy past
so hard to revisit: how they really were,
the things they valued, obstacles *we* faced.
I can only half imagine how it was
to be a girl like you in the early days.

Pillow talk covered most of that I know
but in this monochrome, with little art,
the photographer in his Coleraine studio
caught the young woman I would know and love:
no speech, no fondly interrupted narrative
but the true nature and the secret heart —

as if I knew it, though you were my wife.
I walked on air but was too often drunk
till shouting started and we came undone
in a foreshadowing of the present grief.
When the crab grabbed and spread within
the chance had long gone to make up and thank

you for your forbearance, your anarchic laugh
and the grey gaze there in the photograph,
grey-blue in real life as it opened up
to wit and gaiety, to undying hope.
Dear ghost, remember me without ill will
as I remember your lost mystery still.

But don't mind me, for the important fact
is this, that you were once uniquely here,
a brief exposure, an exceptional act
performed once only in our slower lives
with your blue gaze and your longer hair
now ash for ever in the long sea waves.

Here in Tenerife

Winds light and easterly, decks damp with dew!
Provisioning here in Tenerife, he knew
he was on course, already on his way
to the riches of Chipangu and Quinsay.
Out there his cloud-sailed heaven ships
would find warm anchorage — perhaps;
out there beyond the shining sea
there would be cinnamon, antimony
and nightingales like Córdoba in May.

What if he'd lingered here and found only
aloe, cactus, a black beach? What if
he'd got no farther than this smoky cliff?
Dark ranges soared in the distance.
Would women hold him fast as long before,
or a bad omen, or persistent mist,
so his discoveries weren't out but in —
not gold and spices as in travel lore
but a soul voyage to the interior . . . ?

Goodbye, Columbus. Dogs turn from the tide
uninterested in new worlds, unexcited by
the thought of continents beyond the sky,
and light fading from rock and wrack
gives rise to a dead reckoning.
Day closes quickly at this latitude
as I too return the way I came
and gas brackets like planets climb
a shadowy path back up to the coast road.

The History Train

The present generation sees everything clearly.
　　　　　　　— Gogol, *Dead Souls*

The one-thirty p.m. from Petersburg to Moscow
flashes past meadow, Gazprom and dusky forest
lit only by a twilight candle glow
in the days of revolution and civil war —
a dim vigil for history going sour,
the haunting spectre of a future lost;

and a thicket of aerials up an antique lane.
The ghostly whipped spire of a basilica,
spun blue and white, points to an arctic sky
as in the wilder days of Dostoevsky.
A tiny red light flickers off and on
like somebody smoking at a window sill

or a plane circling to land at Domodedovo.
No leaves left on suburban maple trees.
At the terminal a chill November breeze,
north-easterly, disperses the first snow,
white flurries hesitating too above
the crimson historic plaza where Lenin lies.

What history? Not the driven ones who work
at the huge desks, not strategy, not the dark
intrigues of the *ne kulturny* oligarch
so much as the slow thought of unknown powers,
wind stirring the wheatfields and wildflowers,
and the recurrent music of exemplars —

old folksong, Glinka and his first tutor
fresh from the west, magician of the keyboard,
tone poet of ice tinkle and frozen rain,
his slight sounds deliberate as thaw water

dropping at night, mysterious Field who 'Dead
in Moscow' from a surfeit of champagne.

Daily frustration and vindictive hunger
only intensified the songbirds' fever,
'Aesopian' in its deeply mined obliquity.
Sun dimmed and garden dripped; funereal weather
waited and listened for their silvery cry.
What doesn't kill you makes you stronger.

Icons, tractors, and this devotional urge
lives on in the profitable post-modern era:
dead souls still glistening like caviare,
the unrealized lives of Black Sea sturgeon
issuing finally in a playground song,
miraculous faces of the post-Soviet young.

The last survivors of the difficult years
have faces worn by hardship and lined by tears.
It's thanks to these, the sombre ones who suffered,
that the bright students can sip designer coffee.
'Let's go to the movies!', Voznesensky says;
but films are boring and inane these days.

Palinurus

Condemned to linger in the years ahead
with other souls of the unburied dead
rustling like autumn leaves blown
to the cold roar of smoky Acheron,
we waited there, so many leaves,
so many shadows of our former selves.

A seasoned helmsman, eyes fixed on the night
but sprinkled with a starry dew, sight
dim with somnolence, I'd relaxed my grip;
unnoticed by the rest I slept and slipped
into a dark sea calmer than most,
to be washed up on an unfamiliar coast.

Was there a reason? Many theories fit:
I had a blackout on the night I quit,
Juno required the forfeit of a life
so that the many might be safe,
I'd lost faith in Aeneas and this quick
defection seemed the simplest course; in fact,

wanting no more of the great expedition
I chose obscurity and isolation —
childish perhaps but there you are.
On an unfriendly, now a friendly shore
I lie at last in a grave above the sea,
my bad name a notorious promontory.

Montaigne

Que sçais-je?

Since lately I renounced administration
to spend my time in idle speculation
I've been astonished by the fantasies
an open mind can spin on its dark days;
but a hoof clicks below and an autumn sun
dazzles the live flow of the Dordogne.

I can do nothing without gaiety —
still there despite the death of Boétie.
If one book bores me I pick up another,
skimming and skipping. I would rather
shit like a gent than trouble my digestion
tackling a merely theoretic question.

Some have withdrawn in hopes of a mystique,
others in horror at the great mistake
of this mad century, its religious hate.
Knowing yourself you know the human fate.
What do *I* know? Only immediate things.
I think and write as the bird sings;

for mine is a lazy, self-amusing style,
not grim and purposeful as at Port-Royal.
A thought comes like a raindrop, a slow phrase
like a cloud formation or a September breeze.
I make nature my study as I grow old,
unknowing to the last, in the known world.

Dreams of a Summer Night

The girls are quiet now in the house upstairs.
Still bright at ten with no need of music
on local habitations, tile and brick,
as the moon rises like a magic lamp
hung in a thorn bush and the sun retires
beyond the Bandon River; but I put on
young Mozart's Oboe Concerto, K.314,
the opening bit, in search of a nice tune —
and find it straight away, quick and exact,
the broken silence of the creative act.
Strangely, after the gold rush and the slump,
what remains is a great sense of relief.
Can we relax now and get on with life?
Step out and take a deep breath of night air
in peace, not always having to defer
to market forces, to the great hegemony,
the global hurricane, the rule of money?
High over Innishannon a single star
on the woods of this unthickly wooded shore.
Can we turn now to the important things
like visible scents, how even silence sings?
How we grew frolicsome one sunny June
some sixty years ago at Cushendun
in our young lives of clover, clock and cloud,
the first awakenings under a northern sky
heartbreaking in its extremity? 'One day
the old grow young,' as the old rock star said.

The first movement — *aperto*, open, frank —
declares its candour with a lively run
of oboe riffs; *adagio*, and we think
of the proactive soul in wind and wood
before revisiting the original mood
though more maturely, having lived meanwhile.
It's far from what Said meant by late style

since it was written by a twenty-year-old;
but I'm late listening, taking it all in
like a dreamt 'gentle concord' in the world.
Drilling for oil and war we seldom register
the resilient silence strewn about our toes
and under our very noses: thyme and sage,
mushroom and violet, briony, briar rose
and other elfin species. Soppy, I sniff
inchoate presences in the dim, substantive
trance of a summer night, its peace and quiet,
remembering poetry is a *real* mirage
in an unreal world of cash and babble,
ringtone and car alarm, and remains 'a point of
departure not from reality but to it' —
wherein lies one function of the poet,
to be instrumental in the soul's increase.
During the May rising they used to say
«*Prenez vos désirs pour la réalité;
l'imagination au pouvoir!*» These very reasonable
demands are even more urgent for us today
trying to save ourselves from corporate space,
from virtuality with its image crime,
and Mozart from the ubiquitous pop sound:
fiddle and flute, soft oboe and clarinet,
the next best thing to silence in the mind,
that scarce but still renewable resource.
The young produce the liveliest work of course
but soon enough it's *Wild Strawberries* time,
age and experience, the lost summer house,
girls on a jetty, 'the old sunlit face'.

There was a week of dreams for some reason,
some Kafkaesque and some more seasonable:
a concrete labyrinth with no obvious exit,
a maze of corridors, little natural light,

gruff notices prohibiting this and that,
no eating, drinking, smoking, and don't laugh,
surly administrative and security staff.
Alarms went off at intervals. Doors were shut
and windows, where there were windows, unopenable;
from secret offices a mysterious mumble
qualifying the air-conditioned silence:
Genetics, Human Resources, Behavioural Sciences.
Someone had proved the soul doesn't exist
and wiped out any traces of the past;
all were in danger but it faded fast
at the last minute, only to be replaced
by animations, eyes in a twitchy forest,
oak limbs outgrabbing, knuckles whitening, rock
speaking, Rackham *púcas* at face and neck.
These vanished too; then an erotic bower
snowed in by a warm leaf-and-petal shower
around the long ears and the bristling back.
She lay there in soft focus, her bright eye
moist with provocation; but just as I . . .

So many quiet shores 'bleared, smeared with toil',
there's nowhere for a sticky duck to hide
from the unchecked invasion of crude oil
dumped on the sand by a once friendly tide;
and if they drill here what else do we gain
but a bonanza for an acquisitive crowd
of blow-hard types, determined, garish, loud?
Would we ever get our old lives back again?
Gossip is history, history is gossip —
the locals talking in a hardware shop
about Tom Barry, James II, Marlborough
or that torpedo from a German sub,
the opening wine bar and the closing pub,
the pharmaceutical giant at Dunderrow,

its ethics, working conditions and so on,
a proposal to dig the whole town up again
for fibre optics and more 'information'
now on the table at the Kinsale borough
council and more than likely to go through.
'All politics is local', right where you are.
Communities are the real vehicles of power
not merely its last points of application
or they should be, says Amit Chaudhuri;
water and gas have first consideration
as every pre-Socratic thinker knew.
You hear a different music of the spheres
depending where you sit in the concert space,
so this is the centre of the whole creation:
important or trivial, it all finishes here
on your own starlit doorstep. It could be worse.

A boreal sun, white nights of Petersburg!
The never fading gleam of Tír na nÓg!
But you can have too much of shiny things.
The dark has its own wisdom, its own owl wings,
for this is when the spirits come out to play
and the grim ghosts we daren't admit by day.
Nacht und Träume: geese dreaming of maize,
old Siggi's youngest crying out for 'stwawbewwies',
the entrepreneur with his elaborate schemes,
love dreams, exam dreams and anxiety dreams
'over-interpreted as they need to be.
I had a patient once . . .' But even he
granted the mystery of autonomous art,
those strange impulses circuiting the brain,
the plays of Shakespeare, symphonies of Mozart.

Eleven and still light. No more music now
except for night and silence round the place.

Gazing into the past I hear once more
fathers and uncles back from a won war
and see 'the ice-cream on the pier', the rain
and windy picnics laid out under the brow
of the Cave Hill, Belfast laid out below —
then jump-cut to the dreams, vivid but short,
scaring us as they did when we were ten:
child murder in *Macbeth*, wolves at the door,
the dizzying height and the obscure disgrace,
indictments for a guilt we seldom face.
Sometimes you're hauled before a midnight court,
women presiding, to face charges of
failure in generosity, patience, love
and finer feeling. Often the chief judge
condemns you roundly to a change of heart
and sends you down abruptly for an age
of solitary. Read me the riot act again
in the grave, measured tone you used to restrain
my frantic idiocies. The least *I* can do
is praise your qualities the one way I know
now that I mourn, as here, your grace and poise,
your pungent wit, the laughter in your eyes,
the buoyant upbeat, the interior light
and those odd melancholy moments when
your head would close down with fastidious pain
at a world too coarse and tragic to be borne.
Aspiring spirit, late in finding rest
and harmony, may you have peace at last.
Today in a freak of thought I wondered if
the conservation-of-energy law applies
to souls and promises us eternal life.
At times like this we let ourselves imagine
some substance in the old claim of religion
that we don't die, not really. Don't light residues
commingle with the other starry dead

when our cold ashes in the earth are laid
or scattered on the waves at Port na Spaniagh
and the mad particles begin to spin
like sand grains in the night? Our contribution:
a few good books and a few words of caution.
You the unborn, the bright ones who come later,
remember we too sparkled in the sun,
burst on the shingle, perished underwater,
revolved our secrets in the vast oceans
of time, and live on in our transmigrations.

And you, old friend, Brancusi's 'Sleeping Muse',
who saved me when I'd nothing left to lose,
I can still wish for what you wish for too:
'the amazing truth 'tis no witchcraft to see',
refreshed tradition, lateral thought, a new
world politics and a disabused serenity.
These summer mornings I get up at five,
biro in hand, surprised to be still alive,
grateful for all the clichés and beguiled
by the first birdsong, the first light, the wild
relationship of water and cloud kingdoms
shaping our wishes and our waking dreams.
It's late, so lights out even as a last glow
still lingers on the gardens, on roof and rock:
mid-June now and it's never completely dark
but vague, ambrosial, metamorphic, slow
as if some happy mischief is at work
in the mist-pearly undergrowth below,
transfiguring the earth from dusk to dawn.

The moon floats from a cloud and two dogs bark;
the anthropomorphic trees are trees again,
the human forms recover their wood-grain
and the prehensile skins of hand and groin

revert, the limbs to branches, hair to leaves
as they resume their old arboreal lives.
The girls are fast asleep in the rooms above.
Back here from dreamland with a dewy leaf
to keep me right and ward off disbelief,
I await the daylight we were born to love:
birds at a window, boats on a rising wave,
light dancing on dawn water, the lives we live.

All but two of these poems appear, some in slightly different versions, in *New Collected Poems* (The Gallery Press, 2011). 'Palinurus' and 'Montaigne' were first published in *The Flying Boats* (2014), a limited edition.